True Riches

by

Mary B. Gingerich

True Riches

by
Mary B. Gingerich
16847 Creek Road
Nashwauk, MN 55769

ISBN: 978-1-60126-108-3
Library of Congress Number: 2008927840

All photographs taken by Carol Gingerich
or Justin and Elliot Mullet unless otherwise noted.

Cover photograph taken by Elliot Mullet.

Printed by
Masthof Press
219 Mill Road
Morgantown, PA 19543-9516
www.masthof.com

With Dedication to . . .

My loving husband
who was a constant and faithful companion
for our 45 special years together.

To each of our God given children
who were, and still have a very special
place in my heart and life.

Our six grandsons and two granddaughters
who have brought so much joy to our lives.
And to our dear friends
who are a constant source of blessing!

A Special Place

They work with willing hearts and hands
    Their place in life to fill.
And many times they lift the load
    Of those who climb uphill.

They help the ones with family cares
    And give their time and love.
When others can't, they fill the gap;
    A blessing it does prove!

They work for God—at home, abroad,
    More free to come and go;
I think God's work would crippled be
    Without the seed they sow!

The writer, Paul, says it is good
    To remain in this "state;"
And give full service to the Lord
    Instead of to a mate.

If God has called you to this place,
    In heaven there will be
A special place for those who gave
    Their lives so faithfully!

For Friends

We thank you, God, for friends,
Those lives who've touched our own,
By whose influence sweet
Our souls have richer grown.

Their understanding love,
The confidences true,
And their forgiveness, warm,
Remind me, Lord, of You!

How great Thy wisdom, Lord,
That bountifully sends
The blessed, cherished gift
Of kind and loving friends!

Try It!

A little act of kindness
A little helpful deed
A happy smile of sunshine
A friend to one in need . . .
Will make more pleasant feelings
And chase away the frown;
This cure-all has been proven
And works—the whole year 'round!

The Gift of Friends

Friends mean, Oh, so many things;
    How good that God has given
Friends who care and share and love
    As o'er life's sea we're driven!

Warm thoughts seem to flood my heart,
    As friends pass through my mind.
Each one in a special way
    Has blessed my life, I find!

There are times when these dear friends
    Cannot my longing fill
Yet the friend of all the friends
    Is standing by me still.

Everywhere I turn He shows
    He cares in countless ways.
Thank God for the gift of friends,
    And Best of Friends be praised!

True Riches

I'm glad the things in life which count,
That really are worthwhile,
Cannot be bought with wealth or fame,
Are never out of style.

The love of Christ within the heart,
His Word, a Treasure rare;
Forgiveness clean, to start anew,
The joy of answered prayer!

To have a husband's tender love
And warmth of homey ties;
The wonder of a new-born babe,
The stars in children's eyes.

The crimson flash of winging bird,
The fresh, new start of day,
The beauty of the out-of-doors—
The peace it gives away.

Contentment of a job well done,
The gift of trusted friends,
Good health, a smile, a kindness shown,
Thy goodness never ends.

I'm rich, dear Lord, I wouldn't trade
For tons and tons of gold.
When I have You, then I have all,
The half has not been told!

Another Year

My glad heart is filled with praises
To our Lord who gave this year.
That He led, we cannot doubt it;
Oh, His presence we hold dear!

When the load seemed much too heavy
And we cried, "Can we go on?"
Only One could give the answer
"I'll be with you 'till life's done."

When we faltered, then He prompted;
When we fell, He lifted up;
When we sinned and asked forgiveness,
He forgave and filled our cup!

Oh, the reservoir of goodness
To my knowledge still untapped!
Old year fades, and New Year opens—
It is like a package wrapped.
Tis a gift of His kind mercy
As He guides along the way;
He gives life and breath and seasons,
And a challenge for each day!

So we take each day that's given,
Knowing not what it may hold.
But we know the Lord who gives it;
That His loving arms enfold!

A Meditation

On my lap Baby Anne cooed as we sang the songs of the church, together with other believers. What a blessing, I thought, to grow up with music that has inspired Christians through the ages. What a privilege to be a part of God's family!

I was reminded of some things that influenced my own growing up years: the hymn sings, Sunday school, young people's meetings, sermons, books, Bible school, church gatherings, the counsel and fellowship of family and friends.

Was it to be this way, that no one person or thing was totally responsible for leading me to the dearest Friend I have or ever will know—Jesus my Lord—so that God would have the glory? Thank You, Lord! Thank You for calling me to You.

And, may Baby Anne's cooing some day be replaced with songs of gratitude . . .

I'm Home!

"I'm home from school," she blithely calls,
"O, Mother, where are you?"
With sparkling eyes she comes to say
What all she now can do.

"I know three words: red, yellow, blue,
And I can count so far.
And for a picture that I drew
My teacher gave a star!

"Red Rover is the game we played;
We had the mostest fun.
And teacher read a story, too.
M-m-m! Are those cookies done?"

Such carefree energy and trust,
This eager small life holds.
I'm glad I am the mother of
A bubbling six-year old!

Relaxation

In the circle of Father's arm,
Such comfort and peace were there!
Her head against his shoulder strong
At the time of our evening prayer.

Busy, active, all day was she,
Engrossed in her own little things.
Now so relaxed in Daddy's arms;
The cares had so soon taken wings.

I, too, am busy all the day
With such needful things to be done,
But find it harder to relax
Than this child, at the setting sun.

Grant me the courage, Lord, to do
The most needful things each day;
Then let completely go, and rest
In your arms, at the close of the day.

Mom

House in one grand disarray,
    The dishes piled up high,
Down to one last pair of socks;
    "Our mother's sick," they sigh.

"No aroma's greeting me
    When coming home from school,
Same old clutter everywhere,
    Most everything seems dull!"

"Where's a shoestring, Mumsy dear?"
    "Can't find my English book!"
"My cap's gone, it had been here!"
    "I'm hungry, what's to cook?"

Have you ever wondered, Mom,
    If you were worth a dime?
Spend a few days sick in bed;
    Your role will seem divine!

The Greatest and the Best

It's a joy being wife and mother
    And homemaker, all in one!
It is a high and noble calling
    Status unequalled by none!

Sometimes it seems overwhelming.
    Demands seem to outweigh time,
Without warning, reversals happen;
    Not many hours are called "Mine."

But I have a trustworthy husband;
    He's in this venture with me,
Together we're working at building
    Young lives for eternity!

These children God gave us are treasures;
    No greater joy could there be,
Than to know they walk in the pathway
    Of Him who can keep them free!

He gives friends to brighten our pathway,
    Sometimes to lighten the load,
Or sharing His Word 'round the table
    To help us all down the road.

What blessings to be in God's family,
    One faith and one Blessed Lord!
And helping each other toward heaven,
    Together with one accord!

The favors of God are so numerous,
    Forgiveness surely is one!
Each separate form of creation
    Declares what our God has done!

We wake up each new day refreshened
    He provides grace for the way;
But greatest and best is Christ's presence,
    We thank God for Him each day!

To a Son

Long ago we wanted a son.
God gave us one, what a joy!
We've watched you grow
Through all these years,
And prayed for you, our Boy.

We hurt when you are hurting, son.
And glad when you are glad.
And trust that as manhood you face,
You'll count the joys you've had.

And look to God to guide you through
The days and years to be,
And help some other lads to find
The Lord, who set you Free!

Our Daughters

He places them in our hands, for time,
    A trust of loving care,
The pattern and design are His,
    A choice, unique and rare.

We need to feed, to care for them,
    Provide their clothes each day,
But solid food and pinafores
    Will not endure for aye.

God has a plan for each of them
    And we would guide the way
To Him Who lived, died, rose again,
    And trust He'll be their stay.

But this is a "together" task,
    You need us, we need you,
So Daughters . . .
    Let's join hearts and hands,
    Until our journey's through.

'Mid Common Things

"Dear Lord, as I go through this day
Give me Your strength and grace," I pray.

Then I begin my daily chores;
To clean a bit, and sweep the floors.

The clothes to wash, some beds to make;
A lunch to pack, and cake to bake.

For baby care, write letters too;
To kiss a bruise, and tie a shoe.

A knock is heard, then baby's cry!
"Your grace, Dear Lord, for me," I sigh.

He whispers soft His Word to me:
"Sufficient grace I have for Thee!"

The caller leaves, my work goes on.
But in my heart now dwells a song.

For I have found 'mid common things
That as I work, my heart can sing;

And pray to Him Who lovingly
In His kind grace, hath "holpen" me.

• • •

I Need You

I lost a little key
And it frustrated me!
Alerting me anew—
How much, Lord, I need you
In all of life;
Even in the tiniest situations!

Valentine Special

Paste on kitchen table,
    Clippings on the floor,
Tell-tale crayon markings,
    Fingerprints galore!
Bits of lace and ribbon,
    Tissue paper fine,
Who has such devotion
    For St. Valentine?

Row of shining faces,
    Chores done up first rate,
What could that be showing
    'Neath our dinner plates?
Ah, the spell is broken,
    Cupid's darts ring true;
"You're the best, dear Daddy!"
    "Mother, I love you!"

In His Hand

"Twas sunshine, yes, the sky was blue,
    The blooming flowers smiled;
My heart could sing for all was well—
    God gave to us a child.

A tender, little, loving babe
    He'd given to our care.
She brought glad rays of sunshine,
    And made our lives more fair.

Then sudden clouds of sickness came,
    The rays of sunlight fled.
"I do not think that she will live,"
    The doctor softly said.

She will not live! How could it be?
    My thoughts were in a whirl.
Just yesterday she played and cooed,
    Our darling baby girl.

Then, as the anxious moments passed,
    We waited helplessly
And watched her tiny suffering form
    In silent agony.

But there was One who also stood
    Unseen, yet very near.
Her precious life was in His hand—
    He loves the children dear.

The doctors nobly did their part
    Her little life to save;
The nurses worked so faithfully
    As needed care they gave.

Our prayers were mingled with the prayers
    Of loving friends and kin.
Would health be given back to Anne?
    We left it all with Him.

Then one by one the aids were moved:
　　The tubes, the pump, and gear.
New life was surging through her veins,
　　Recovery was near.

I'll always treasure that first smile,
　　Her cry was good to hear.
What joy to see her strength return;
　　It brought us all much cheer.

"She may go home," the doctor smiled.
　　What truth those words revealed:
Thank God! He'd wrought a miracle—
　　Our baby Anne was healed.

Our Role Has Changed

Grandma! Grandpa! Those magic words!
    As in our arms one day
They placed a babe; sweet, soft, and new,
    Our role had changed to stay!

No matter if it's first or eighth,
    The joy of it remains;
A small new life to hold and love,
    A calling God ordained!

It's awesome, too, this place we fill
    In small arms reaching up;
To meet that need, whate're it be,
    In heart as well as cup.

So, "Will you read a story, please?"
    We welcome with delight,
To have them come to spend a day,
    And sometimes for a night.

Yes, discipline and diapering
    Are mostly Mom's and Dad's,
But sharing and caring times make
    Grandparents' hearts so glad!

We thank God for these precious ones,
    His gifts sent from above.
Our prayers surround each one in turn—
    This circle of our love!

• • •

My Desire

I love Thy pure Word, Lord.
Continue to weave it
Into my entire life;
That it may become the
Woof and warp of my being.

The Sweetest Bouquet

With a smile she brings her off'ring
Of first dandelions in Spring,
Though wilted in chubby handclasp
How precious the thoughts it brings!

Other arrangements may dazzle
This is the sweetest, so true!
The wordless, unspoken message
"Grandma, you know I love you!"

Those Golden Years

Due honor rightly goes to those
    Who've walked life's rugged way;
And we do well to hearken to
    The wisdom they convey!

Their words are backed by practiced lives,
    Through good and ill they've come
And, oh, the treasures they can share
    From races bravely run!

These later years are golden years,
    A crown of glory, they,
If found in ways that please the Lord,
    True riches are their pay.

The outward man may slowly dim,
    But inner strength and grace
Is given daily to those saints,
    Who fill their special place!

God planned that we should come this way,
      The day when we were born;
First, childhood, youth, and middle age,
      Then golden years adorn!

Do not apologize, my friends,
      For faltering hands and feet,
You've taught me much! And it is true—
      That old age can be sweet!

• • •

Time Counts!

Tiny seconds, little minutes,
      Hour by hour, and day by day,
Weeks and months and years go swiftly,
      Softly stowing time away.
'Til one day when Time is ended
      Face to face with Christ we'll be
How will we this question answer:
      "Hast thou spent this Time for me?"

No Age With God

Antiques are things that grow
    More valuable with age;
They may be used and worn,
    Yet antiques are the rage.

The Word, too, puts value
    On graying men of God,
They have much to offer
    Who have life's rough road trod.

Outward man grows feeble;
    His bones ache, vision dims,
May lose teeth and hobble,
    Short on vigor and vim.

All the world grows older;
    The rings increase in trees,
Land becomes less fertile,
    It groaneth with disease.

Things and man keep changing,
    This started at the fall.
But with God, it's different,
    He changeth not at all!

He always was and will
    The same forever be;
Dying men who trust Him
    Will live eternally!

• • •

Rest in the Storm

The hurricane roars wildly,
    But, strangely, in its midst
There is an eye of Calmness
    That through the storm exists!
Life's sore trials come my way
    And rage around my soul,
I find rest and quiet peace
    Within the Shepherd's fold!

Our Life Span, Like a Rose

There are seasons to our life span,
    For our God has planned it so;
First a baby, tiny seedling,
    Pushing up, we watch it grow.

Jesus blessed the little children
    Said we must become like them,
Trusting, loving, and forgiving,
    With a child-like faith in Him.

Next is youth, like tender rosebud,
    With their zeal and energy . . .
"Let no one despise your young age,
    You should an example be."

Middle age now surely follows
    With the height of rose in bloom;
Nurt'ring, building, sharing, working
    For the Lord—those years pass soon.

Golden age brings drooping petals
    Filled with wisdom from years long;
Even though the petals dry up,
    Their sweet perfume lingers on.

One depends upon the other
    For a full rose to become;
Then a lasting fragrance ensures
    When the autumn time is gone.

Each age has some contribution;
    Blessed are they, who heed this truth,
Everyone is so much needed—
    Older, middle, babe, and youth.

Turn the Wick to Him

'Twas the Lord that lit the candle
    Within my longing heart.
His Spirit came to burn within,
    His blessings to impart!

He chose a holder made of clay,
    So nicked and marred with sin;
To place His everlasting flame
    Of love and peace within.

If breezes blow of doubts and cares,
    And fan the flame quite dim,
The only way to health and glow
    Is turn the wick to Him.

'Tis He alone can give the touch
    That sets my heart aflame.
O Master, keep the touch aglow
    Within my earthly frame!

                     – Romans 12:1

The Game of Life

Are we sitting in the bleachers,
Or playing in the game?
Just to observe or to take part,
Are surely not the same.

All can win in this game of Life,
If we participate.
A shouting spectator only
Will not with our Coach rate!

He gave His all to give us life,
His power to o'er come sin.
The Book of Books to chart our course,
So we could run and win!

No U-Hauls There

When some day we'll meet our Jesus,
When we answer that last call,
Then the earth-bound things we've gathered,
Will like melting ice-drops fall!

Our last name won't be important,
And no titles may we claim,
But "Are you washed in Jesus blood?"
Do you bear His precious name?

All riches and the glory
Of this earth seem very cheap,
When compared with lasting treasures,
And eternal traits that keep.

What we have is given to us,
Just to use while here below,
And we'll take no U-Hauls with us
When to heav'n we're called to go!

Such Wonders

When pondering what Jesus has done for me; it doesn't add up or make sense—all the goodness He's showered upon me, He's poured out at His own expense!

Not a thing I've done has deserved His grace, the wooing and love were from Him. O the depth and the riches of God's love; He took me in all of my sin!

Giving His life on the cruel, harsh cross; left heaven that I may go free; breaking the shackles that once held me fast. Praise Him! There is now peace for me!

He rose victorious that I too may rise! In heaven He's pleading for me. There's no one in all of this whole wide world, who could do such wonders as He!

He's Always There

The sun is always shining,
    Though clouds may hide its face.
All the rainy, misty days
    Cannot its shine erase.

When storm clouds gather o'er us
    And everything looks gray,
When all our hopes are shattered;
    There seems to be no day.

Remember God is by you,
    His love is always there;
And all the earthly troubles
    Will never change His care.

By faith we trust the Master
    In sunlight or in shade;
"Lo, I am with you always"
    "Fear not, Be not afraid!"

Thy Power Through Me

Before my thinking time
    You planned for me,
Your thoughts spanned now, and through
    Eternity!

You've long range plans for me
    How short my sight;
My efforts seem so small
    To Your great might!

But wonder of it all,
    Though frail I be,
'Tis not my power, but Thine
    That works through me.

Redeemed, reclaimed, my life
    I trust to You;
The Present, and the Past,
    The Future—too.

The Precious Blood

The Blood is my hope.
The Blood is my gain.
If it weren't for the Blood
Then my sins would remain.

The Blood washes clean,
The Blood makes me whole.
It's the Blood of the Lamb
That brings peace to my soul.

The Blood gives me life.
The Blood gives me power.
The precious Blood Christ spilt
Is my song and my tower!

All Things Through Him

To know God is to truly live,
    And through this truth we pray—
Creator of the Universe,
    Our Light, our Guide, our Way.

We bow before Him, "Lord of Life,"
    None other fills this place,
The Saviour of our very souls
    He bought by blood and grace.

We need to keep our hearts attune,
    Confess our sins to Him;
And as we focus on His love,
    Our view of self grows dim.

But life at times is difficult,
    The load seems hard to bear.
We may not feel Him close at times
    And even doubt His care.

God is bigger than our problems,
    Far greater than our woe,
And so we plead His promise of
    "I'll never let you go!"

When we have failed or get the blues,
    "O Lord, forgive," we cry,
Like Paul, we must forget and press
    To gain that prize on high!

Each one of us has handicaps,
    Our tears may overflow,
He gives us strength, if we but seek
    To overcome below.

How often when we call to Him,
    He speaks by His own Word,
And this gives us the confidence,
    He's there! And He has heard!

God gave the task for us to bring
        Others to Him in prayer.
It changes happ'nings, hearts, and lives
        And blesses those who care!

In asking God we must believe
        That His choice is the best;
Submitting to His plan for us
        Brings peace and quiet rest.

True prayer then is offering Him
        Our whole self and our will.
Then all things will be possible.
        Lord, teach thy servants still!

I thank God who created us
        In such a way that He
Alone can fill our longings deep,
        And set our spirits free!

Inexpressible

The truth that You do love me, Lord
    Just thrills me o'er and o'er!
How can I praise You as I ought?
    Mere words cannot adore.

I lay myself down at Your feet,
    My heart, my life, is Thine,
It's all that I can give Thee, Lord.
    It is no longer mine.

No chorus here has perfect praise
    But heaven, O glad thought!
When in Thy Presence I can sing
    And praise Thee as I ought!

His Specialty

Out of the depths of my soul I cried:
    My heart was broken and beat.
Helpless, in need, and no where to turn
    My soul bowed low at His feet.

"How can any good come out of this
    O Lord?" My aching heart cried;
"It seems entirely impossible,
    For all's failed that has been tried."

I'd quite forgotten the specialty
    Of our Loving Lord and King
How He works to His glory and praise
    Any broken life or thing!

As this precious truth dawned on my heart
    And spread through my seeking soul;
His blessed assurance gave me peace,
    His Truth once more made me whole.

Paradox?

Thou dwellest God, in Heav'n above
And yet, Thou leadest me in love!

At God's right hand, O Christ, Thou art
And yet, You live within my heart!

The Holy Spirit, One with Thee
And yet He fills and comforts me!

Thy living Word, inspired of old
And yet, the same, sweet message holds!

The world rejects Thee, to Thy face
And yet, You love—Amazing Grace!

"Incredulous!" Is what they say
In this our "wise" and "modern" day.

O keep me from disdain's acquiesce,
And Lord, my meager faith increase!

Not by Bread Alone

Man cannot live by bread alone,
    The kind with wheat and rye,
But every word that God has given—
    Tis manna from on high!

It has choice portions of good food,
    If we but dig and find;
And O, the way it nourishes
    The heart and soul and mind!

But if I miss the helping that
    He daily has for me,
I soon find weakness creeping in
    And stiffness of the knee!

Rich food it is, this Word of God
    Health nutrients that make whole,
The only vitamins around
    To save a sin-sick soul!

Ho! Everyone that hungers for
    The food that has no price;
It satisfies and fills your needs,
    Ah! Does not this entice?

The Truth Will Stand

When it seems wrong is in the right
    And sin has the upper hand;
The Word of God is still the same
    The truth will always stand!

The promises are just as sure,
    The judgments still remain;
And tho' the world seeks to destroy,
    The truth will be our gain!

Down through the ages man has sought
    An easy way, his own.
But in the end he always finds
    The Word is truth, alone!

Photo credit: John Pennover

The Love of God

The love of God:
    It fills,
    And thrills,
    Then spills
Into the lives around us.

    It glows
    And grows
    Then Flows
To others that surround us.

    It feels,
    And deals,
    Then heals
Our hearts that would be
        straying.

    It weeps
    To reap
    And keep
The souls that are decaying.

    It cares
    To bear
    And share
The blessed gospel story.

    Who heeds
    It feeds
    Then leads
Thru this life into glory.

THE LOVE OF GOD!

Here I Come Again

Here I come again, dear Lord,
    As many times before.
I've tasted of Your Goodness
    But yearn to know You more.

You've showered me with blessings
    And peace there is inside;
Yet somehow there's a longing
    For more, I must confide.

I know we'll never grasp
    The full extent of grace,
Until we see You, Saviour
    In heaven, face to face.

Precious Lord, I need You now
    Just draw me closer still;
Day by day fill Thou my need
    Of going deeper still.

My Heart's an Altar

My heart's an altar, Lord,
    Thou dwellest there.
From heav'n You came to me—
    Thy love to share!

Alone, or in the crowd
    I may commune;
Among the pots and pans—
    This sacred room.

I cannot comprehend
    This mystery;
But I believe Thy Word
    Fulfilled in me.

Forever Forgotten

When God has moved in and forgiven,
He clears the soul of its sin;
Forever that sin has been cancelled—
No more remembered by Him!

How oft do we find ourselves guilty
And do what God cannot do,
And take sins which Christ's blood has covered,
And bring them back to full view!

Forgetting then, goes with forgiving
Our sins and others sins, too,
God's mercy will surely flow through us,
If Christ's way we will pursue.

Faces

What kind of face do you wear
    When going down the street?
Does it make a difference
    On whom you chance to meet?

Some folks have a drawerful
    To pull out as they go;
Smiling, frowning, murm'ring ones,
    Depends on whom they know!

When Christ cleans up the inside
    You need not mask your face.
He gives pleasantness for all
    At any time or place!

The Greatest Miracle

We saw it happen and a wonder it is;
A girl bent for troubles' deep side.
The teachers and parents had nearly despaired
Every rule in the book was tried.

But little by little the Gospel took hold
'Til one night she answered God's call.
For she, like the rest of us needed to come
To the blood-washed cross with her all.

They call this a miracle performing age
Such wonders unheard of before.
But the heart changing miracle Christ performs
Is the greatest miracle . . . and more!

Now!

Time is too short to idle away
    In gossip, so hurtful and trite.
Someone is needing our love today
    Let's *go* while the moment is ripe!

Things we would hoard will vanish with time,
    Shall the needy world die at our door?
Heartsick and homeless, in anguish they pine,
    Let's *give* from our bountiful store.

Christ seeks now, our sincere devotion,
    Tomorrow's too late to obey,
He's longing to fill every portion
    Let's *be* while it's yet called today.

Stand Still and See

The Red Sea was before them;
    Behind them was the foe.
They left their all in Egypt,
    Now this—no place to go!

They cried out in great distress
    "Why did you bring us here?
Egypt's slaves we'd rather be
    Than die in this great fear!"

Moses said, "Fear not, stand still
    And see God's saving power.
Egypt soon will know Who is
    The Strong and Mighty Tower!"

The world is close behind us;
    Our Red Sea lies before.
The walls are high, the waters deep,
    There is no open door.

Then we cry out unto the Lord,
    "Ah, whither shall we go?
The way is closed before us,
    Behind us is the foe!"

Then comes a voice so tender,
    "Stand still and look to Me.
I'm able to deliver;
    Completely trust in Me!"

And, as we wait, He also says
    "Go forward, child, in faith."
This is the true believer's life:
    What promises He hath!

God's Doors

Have you ever had a door
        That seemed to open wide
Close up as you were ready
        To take a step inside?

I tremble at what might be,
        If doors that I thought best
Would have yielded to my will
        Without His loving test.

I thank Him for reproving,
        That He gave faithfully,
When I have gone through a door
        That was not meant for me.

I'm glad God in His wisdom,
        Ahead can clearly see;
And opens up or closes
        The door that's best for me.

So may I not be hasty
        To ope' the door of choice;
But wait on God to lead me,
        And listen to His voice.

A Personal Matter

We are responsible to God
    For every thought and deed,
The act of choosing right or wrong
    Depends on how we heed.

It is so easy just to think,
    "If only he . . . or she
Would act a little differently,
    Then I could better be!"

"If circumstances in my life
    Were of a different kind,
Perhaps my service for the Lord
    Much easier I'd find!"

It seems that Eve and Adam, too
    Had tried to shift the blame.
But God dealt individually
    As He called each by name.

To God, a personal account,
    Each one of us must give;
Not how my neighbor's life, but mine
    In honesty was lived.

King of Kings, His Role!

Creator of the universe,
Controller of all time,
Master of the elements,
Our Lord, Man, yet Divine.

The one who fashioned mortal man
And all his needs supplied;
This Jesus, First and Last of all
In love for mankind died!

They had no power but what He gave,
And yet, they chose to kill
The very one who gave them life
God's plan He did fulfill!

The earth did quake, the rocks were split,
The veil was rent in twain,
Darkness concealed the dreadful act;
The Lamb, God's Son was slain!

The graves were opened and saints arose,
Oh, what a day we cry,
But it was there for my own sins
He gave His life to die!

The tomb could not this great one hold,
He shattered death's control,
The mighty Prince in splendor rose
Now *King of Kings*, His role!

God Needs Such Men Today

People talk about commitment
    To many things these days;
Allegiance to a cause or cure
    In devious sorts of ways.

It may be for a day or month,
    And maybe even years;
It brings some satisfaction—
    Allays some temporal fears.

Commitment to Christ and His cause
    Is for a life-time through.
To take His cross, a daily choice
    Means self-denial, too.

One goal, we have,—to please the Lord;
    Devoted we must be.
We are not fit if we look back
    And sail sins' luring sea.

As Daniel purposed in his heart—
    It was no picnic then!
Through ridicule, passed lions' jaws,
    God's power led that man!

Many godly men have since then
    Stood steadfast to the last,
They sought not praise nor men's reward
    With God their die was cast!

Others, too, begin the right way
    Wanting what God can do.
But trials, tests, and life's pleasures
    Trip them up, and they're through!

Steady, faithful, ready plodders,
    Single mind to obey,
Drawing from the Source who saved them,
    God needs such men today!

Why Compare?

"If only I could sing like Kate
    Or draw like sister Sue—
And what I'd give to look like Barb!
    Or speak as well as you."

"If Bill would manage well like Joe
    And John like Mike could teach . . .
I wish that Brother Dan with force
    Like Pastor Bob, could preach."

Comparing us among ourselves
    We lose such blessings rare,
For hasn't God formed each of us
    With thought and loving care?

A special place to each He's given,
    That no one else can fill,
And to compare—we may decline
    To follow in His will.

If we are then divinely called,
    We need to thankful be
And recognize each others' good
    And work in harmony.

Looking to Jesus

The thief on the cross
    Acknowledged his need,
And he entered heaven
    The day he was freed.

Now often we look
    On the outward, I fear.
And miss the heart's cry
    Of a seeker sincere.

• • •

These are two commandments
    From which we must not swerve,
"To love the LORD with all our heart,
    Him only must we serve."

"To love our neighbor as ourself,"
    We also need to do.
Whatever else there is besides;
    They all hang on these two.

The Church, God's Garden

A garden of flowers,
    O, what a delight!
The blend of all colors
    A beautiful sight!

Tall asters, shy violets,
    Sweet Williams in bloom,
Petunias and fuchsia,
    The lilac's perfume!

Morning glory climbing,
    The daffodil's nod,
Geranium's bright colors,
    The artwork of God!

Some are for the background,
    Tall, strong to be seen,
While some are the border,
    But, most in-between.

Each church is a garden
    Arranged by God's hand;
All flowers of His grace—
    A beautiful blend!

Each member so fashioned
        With delicate skill,
Like flowers to blossom
        And bloom in His will!

The daisies and roses
        Cannot be the same,
Neither can those be, who
        Are called by God's Name.

And each fills a place of
        Most infinite worth;
Harmonizing in Christ,
        Showing His love on earth!

This garden on earth has
        Much work to be done—
Of planting and hoeing,
        But life in the Son!

Hidden Worth

Eliab, tall, and eldest son,
Him, surely God would choose.
Not so; man seeth outwardly,
His heart, God did refuse.

So one by one they failed the test,
For "God does not choose these."
Then Samuel called for David, meek,
His heart the Lord did please.

How oft we judge by trivial things.
What means? Has he degrees?
Which family tree? And he should be
Well-groomed and speak with ease!

But God desires hidden worth
In motive, thought, and soul.
He seeketh such to serve Him, who
By Christ have been made whole!

With Blood-dripped Love

When we try to size up people
    Who come along our way,
And pour them into our own mold
    And put them there to stay . . .

And if we find the form is wrong
    And our style won't agree,
We tend to chop and cut to size
    And cause much injury.

Ah, but our Lord does not do this!
    He takes us as we are;
And then with gentle voice and hand
    He molds us with great care.

He does not discipline, then leave,
    To let us hurt alone.
But faithfully He gives us grace
    'Till we have wiser grown.

He asks not what our last name is,
    Or which side of the tracks,
Or if we're coming out on top,
    Or in man's eyes we lack?

With blood-dripped love He takes us
    Without partiality.
Oh Lord, love through the Brotherhood
    And love like this through me!

Jesus Is Here!

Are you lonely today
    because no one came?
        Jesus is here!

Or are you bowed down
    with constant dread pain?
        Jesus is here!

Has someone you trusted
    gone back on his word?
        Jesus is here!

You asked for something
    and you haven't been heard?
        Jesus is here!

You showed someone kindness
    and you were refused?
        Jesus is here!

Or has life bought hard things
    which you did not choose?
        Jesus is here!

• • •

No matter how heavy the load that you bear;
He's promised to guide you and carry your care.
He hurts when you hurt and He feels what you feel.
He knows all your weakness, He surely will heal.

Just talk to Him now as you would to a friend,
Tell Him all about it, His ear He will lend.
If forgiveness you need—then He will forgive.
He will give you peace and a purpose to live.

He may not take all of your troubles away,
But He will be with you, He promised to stay!
His arms will uphold you, He'll carry you through.
And many more blessings He has promised too!

• • •

He Broke Death's Claim

I wonder how Barabbas felt
    When the guard turned the key;
And said that Jesus took his place—
    He now could go scot-free?

Ah, death had stared him in the face;
    He had deserved his fate!
And now the gift of Life was given,
    No strings attached—just take!

I wonder how Barabbas felt?
    I think I know in part.
I, too, was bound in chains of sin
    And dark doubts ruled my heart.

The resurrection power with which
    Christ rolled death's claim away;
Has broken down that wall of sin
    And He came in to stay!

It is this power that keeps me now,
    His blood that washes me.
How can we find words to describe
    This Gift, so rich and free?

Oh, praise the Name of Him who lives
    And reigns forever more!
Who broke death's claim and made a way
    For us to Heaven's shore!

And some day soon He's coming back
    To take His children home—
The praises of the raptured ones
    Will go forever on!

Deception's Wiles

Deception comes in subtle ways,
Disguised in robes of right;
With acts of kindness, 'pretend love,'
All served with sweet delight!

With half-truths found on flow'ry paths,
Of reas'nings which seem wise,
Soft lights and music to allure
And still a heart's deep cries.

To rebel hearts who want their way,
It lends a listening ear;
Then wrests the truth to make it say
Whatever they will hear.

It's possible to read God's Word
And hear it day by day—
Yet James warns, we will be deceived
If we do not obey.

Seeds of deception quickly grow
In beds of discontent,
And watered by ungratefulness,
They grow with downward bent.

It may not show till judgment time,
Such is deception's way;
"Have we not done much in Thy Name?"
But Jesus turns away.

Lord, keep me covered with the blood,
Renew it day by day,
And as you show the truth to me,
Quickly, I will obey!

May I remember that the Word
And Spirit do agree,
With Father and with Son alike;
To heed them will make free!

On Thoughts

A tiny thought came winging by
    The sunny, cheerful, kind.
It nestled in a ready place
    Somewhere within my mind.

It grew—that lovely little thought
    And filled my heart with song.
And those I touched were also blessed,
    Our ties were made more strong.

Another day, a shaded thought
    Sought entrance to my heart;
And, thoughtlessly, I let it in
    To lodge its poison dart.

The ugly thought, it also grew
    From just a tiny seed,
Becoming next some unkind words
    And then, an unkind deed.

So let us guard the thoughts that come
    And try them, every one;
The goodly ones may enter in
    The ugly ones—send on!

A Sweet Delight

Count no task too small,
Or worthless in His sight;
If done for Christ alone,
You'll find a sweet DELIGHT!

• • •

One Moment's Choice

Judas freely walked with Jesus
    And shared His love from day to day.
Yet temptation's strong hold gripped him
    And with one kiss threw all away!

O, the weight of that one moment!
    Yes, life or death were in that choice;
Had he known the consequences
    When he yielded to Satan's voice?

Life has many weighty choices,
    As we, each travel on our way:
O, Dear Master, keep us near thee,
    Lest we, in weakness, go astray!

The Miracle

Deceitful, yes, above all things,
And hopelessly in need;
The heart without the risen Lord
Is barren soil indeed!

It seeks by many ways and means
To hush the still, small voice;
While there is One Who stands without
To plead, and wait its choice.

Then in despair the heart is turned
His mercy to employ.
And lo, it springs into a well
Of never-ending joy!

Too Many Hypocrites?

"I won't be going to church today,
Too many hypocrites there," you say.

Friend, you don't shop, for some people steal,
And get away with things they conceal?

You do not send your children to school,
For there are those who dare break the rules?

Don't socialize, for some prove untrue?
Ah, Friend, I know those things are not you!

When we stand by our God great and true,
We can't depend on what some don'ts do!

Each person answers for his life, lived;
All will a rating from God receive.

Church, my friend, is the best place to be;
Christ formed it in love for you and me.

Hypocrites there? Good places they go,
Faking the right is their work, you know.

Please don't try avoid hypocrites here,
Or you may ever be with them there!

• • •

Eyesore

"Beholdest thou the tiny mote?
What of thy beam-size sin?"
These searching words that Jesus spoke
Make my heart burn within.

Physician, take the crippling beam;
This critic's "righteous" zeal,
Then, as Thy oil of love flows in
My sister's good reveal.

The Berean Way

We have such easy ways to hear
    The preaching of today;
You just tune in and there it is,
    A smorgasbord, I'd say!

We can hear it while we're dining,
    Or tune in on the run,
It comes all peeled and cored and cut,
    You take your pick, which one?

How often, after listening
    Do we take out the Word,
To read and search, and then compare
    With what we just have heard?

The Bereans took the time to see
    If what they heard was true;
Their plumb-line was the Word of God,
    The rest was all taboo!

They're classed as noble in God's Word,
    No spoon-fed lot were they!
They heard and searched, and then believed
    So we must do today!

The Sermon

"It was as dry as toast today,
    I cannot understand
Why Pastor Brown can't make it clear
    So we could comprehend!"

"Please, may I disagree with you?
    For I have found a clue,
I was searching for an answer
    Which Pastor brought to view."

Why was one blessed, the other not?
    The sermon was the same,
One criticized, the door was shut.
    One sought, the answer came!

Needed!

The nails said to the window panes,
    "We wish that we might be,
So placed like you to clearly shine
    For all the world to see!"

"But here we are, hidden from view,
    Unnoticed day by day;
If we'd drop out, no one would know
    That we had gone away."

The window slightly shuddered then
    At the nails' attitude;
"The value of your spot in life,
    I fear you wrongly viewed!"

"If you would suddenly disappear
    And leave me here alone,
I surely then, would break to bits
    When your support is gone!"

"How could this building have been made
    With only that which shows?
'Disaster' is a fitting word
    Describing such a woe!"

"From solid base to rafters high,
    With many things between;
Much more, you'll notice, is concealed
    Than parts which can be seen."

"The Builder chose which place would be
    The *best* for you and me."
"Thanks, Brother, I feel needed now,
    The truth you helped me see!"

(Taken from I Corinthians 12)

Nature's Wonders!

All around us nature beckons
To enjoy so God designed.
In return we thank and praise Him
As His handiwork we find.

A woodsy path of treasures rare
A partridge's hidden nest,
Shy violets smiling, May flowers too,
Lacy fern fronds at their best.

The many blends of green in spring,
An array of flowering trees,
New growth, like candles on the pines,
And soft wafts of scented breeze.

Some deer along a country road,
And fair mallards by the way.
Marsh marigolds splash of color,
Rare sunsets at the end of day.

The snowshoe rabbit changing dye
To summer brown from all white;
To hear the loon's cry from the lake,
And watch the heron in flight.

The earth's the Lord's and all therein
In wisdom His works abound;
In summertime, vacation time
We perceive Him all around!

On Kingdom Building

How blessed it is to be a part
    Of the kingdom that God has made.
The old and the young work side by side,
    As they build, with the Spirit's aid.

Each one is unique, no two alike;
    Yet striving for one common goal.
One purpose in mind—to please the One
    Through whose blood we have
        been made whole.

When our vision is dimmed because of sin,
    And we lose sight of the Prize;
Then kingdom building comes to a halt,
    The Spirit of unity dies!

How sweet it is when ties are restored.
    Forgiveness and love rules again;
And we serve the Lord and each other
    In God's family made up of men!

Thank You Prayer

Thank you Lord,
       for all the lovely things
       of the great out-of-doors.
What beauty in the blending of colors!

And thank you, Lord, more,
       for the lovely, priceless gift
       of your great self.
The blending of your spirit with mine.

That I may worship Thee!

Magic Autumn

With tint and color Autumn comes
In field and forest deep,
And, wand in hand, she glides along
With magic step and fleet.

She touches every tiny leaf,
With mystic, magic hand.
Then flings her golden hues around
In brilliance, O, so grand!

With lovely tapestries flung high
And low on every bough;
'Tis really God that's passing through
With graceful beauty now.

His Touch

The world that's bathed in moonlight
Has a lovely touch;
The graceless lines of daytime
Have melted with the dusk:

      The scrubby bush
      The scrawny branch
      The loathsome weed
      The withered grass

      Have mellowed with the night.

The heart that's bathed in Christ's love
Is touched with priceless glow;
All sinful deeds now washed away
By cleansing overflow:

      The hateful thought
      The unkind deed
      The thoughtless word
      The selfish way

      Forsaken for the right.

Too Good to Keep

Christmas is not tinsel, holly,
    Or bows and mistletoe.
It is Jesus come from Heaven
    Giving that "inner glow!"

The true, love-Gift that God has giv'n.
    Cannot be tied with string,
But overflows within the hearts
    Of those who know the King!

If your Christmas had no pine tree,
    No parceled gifts from friends;
Would you still rejoice in Jesus
    On whom our joy depends?

O, the Gift that God has given
    Is far too good to keep!
The happiest folks are those who share
    This Good News so complete.

A Priceless Treasure

God's Word is like a treasure chest,
　　All filled with gems so rare.
Its precious contents are revealed
　　To those who seek and care.

Manna from heaven is within,
　　And pearls of greatest price;
The way to live, the way to die,
　　The way to make one wise.

Whoever will may open up,
　　There only is one key,
It's Christ who can unlock the lid
　　To truths that set us free!

So many imitation pearls
　　Are scattered all around;
Folks buy them up and wear them, too
　　And think they're heaven bound.

But Jesus is the Word made flesh,
　　Yes, Jesus is the Key!
He's all the treasures put in "One,"
　　A Priceless Pearl is He!

Whose Slaves Are We?

When God from Egypt led His own,
They had but simple fare;
He asks us, too, to be content
With food and clothes to wear.

If one good food we had for years
For breakfast, dinner, lunch;
I wonder—would we be content
And thank the Lord a bunch?

And wear the same old clothes for weeks,
One month, one year, then two,
Year after year for forty years!
Just think, what would we do?

How would we entertain our friends?
No fancy foods to share;
No talk of new books off the press,
What crafts at that last fair?

We couldn't go on shopping sprees,
No yard or rummage sales,
No malls, flea markets, big chain stores,
Might this bring forth some wails?

God led them through the desert land
To trust Him gratefully,
But they yearned for the good old days
Though they'd in bondage be!

"I'll never leave thee," Jesus said.
We should so thankful be!
Are we becoming slaves to things,
And need to be set free?

Environment or Choice?

The environment was perfect,
No weeds, no thorns, no sin,
So was the couple—not a stain
When God placed them within.

Not a flaw in the arrangement,
God set it up Himself.
They had access to everything,
With perfect mind and health!

O, yes, there was just one small catch,
"Of one tree, do not eat!"
It truly was the best of plans
To make life all complete!

They surely could quite easily cope
In such an ideal place,
No one with whom to disagree
Or shun what you embrace!

And in this lovely garden spot
Just made for One and Two,
Each one was given the free will
Of right or wrong to do.

Then Eve partook and Adam, too,
What sadness reigned that day!
"Twas Eve gave me," "No, was the snake,
That made me go astray!"

But each one had to answer
For the sin that they had done;
They could not blame each other,
But face up to their wrong.

The will to do the right or wrong
Each one this choice must bear,
We must decide, not pass the buck,
As well as that first pair!

The Power of Choice

We do not choose
    Our birth, 'tis true,
But now we choose
    Which way we'll go.

God gives the power
    Of choice to all,
And by it we
    Will rise or fall.

We choose for self
    Or God above,
We choose to hate
    Or live in love.

We choose what thoughts
    Stay in our mind,
To grumble or
    Some beauty find.

We choose to grudge
        Or to forgive,
To speak the truth
        Or two-faced live.

Our choices are
        Like building stones,
And we will reap
        The choices sown.

We cannot blame
        Our Lord or man,
God gives us choice
        And power to stand.

The cross or world?
        Which will it be?
The choice is ours;
        Our destiny!

The Gathering Together

Do not forsake the gathering,
    The manner of some will be such.
His coming is fast approaching,
    We need this assembling so much!

God speaks through the message given;
    How often my soul has been blest,
When a well-known truth was confirmed
    Or sin was revealed to confess!

Speakers may vary in person,
    God uses weak vessels of clay;
The power of His Word ne'er changes
    Its message endureth for aye!

It is a "togetherness" hour
    As we listen and pray and sing;
Worship in one soul and spirit
    To our Saviour and Lord and King!

We need to cherish this privilege;
    At places it's taken away,
And very lives are sacrificed;
    A price they are willing to pay!

(From Hebrews 10:25)

A "Faithful" Crown

Some would splash the front page news
With deeds of world renown.
Others seem to get the prize
When ere it's passed around.

We may seem quite unnoticed,
When we've no gown to wear,
Sometimes wondering how 'twould be
For such a privilege rare!

God has promises enough
For those who are His own;
If we believe and claim them
We need not feel alone.

His living presence to guide
Each day our whole life through;
To find His will and follow,
Gives peace and joy anew!

The world's rewards and riches
Are painf'ly weak and small,
Compared with countless blessings
Of Christ's sweet will and call.

Our desire then would be
Of being found in Him;
If to the end we're faithful,
A crown of life we'll win!

I Am With You to the End

"I'll never leave you," how those words
    Bring sweet comfort to our souls;
In the midst of daily routine,
    That truth does each hour enfold!

When heavy schedules fill the day
    And we're weary to the bone,
Ah, those words "I'm in there with you"
    Bring renewal of their own!

Miles and miles down busy highways
    He has carried us along;
In accidents his care was there,
    Proving a companion strong!

Many friends we have who love us,
     There are some who've gone away;
Christ sticks closer than a brother,
     "Lo, I'm with you, here to stay!"

He's our comfort in our illness,
     When we are too weak to pray,
Giving strength and healing with it,
     Great Physician, without pay!

Thank You, Lord, for this great promise,
     "I am with you to the end."
Yes, we know the One who gave it
     Is our precious, loyal Friend!

Jesus, the Only Way

Some say that there are many ways
    That will in Heaven end—
"Just choose a path that's good for you
    And do the best you can."

Only God, who created us,
    Could give a rightful Way,
For man cannot redeem himself,
    Who sinned, since Adam's day.

God sent His Son to live on earth,
    So He could feel for man,
And then, He suffered death for us,
    But rose to break death's chain!

He is the Only Path to God,
    One Word, the Source of Love.
The Shepherd Good, who daily leads
    Till our life ends above!

He feeds our hungry soul with food,
    The Bread of Life is He!
He is the Door of Heaven's gate,
    The Light that we may see!

He is the Vine to which we cling,
    The only great "I AM!"
The Resurrected, Glorious One,
    God's Sacrificial Lamb!

The other paths all lead to death,
    To think they're right, how odd!
He is the Way, the Truth, the Life,
    Jesus, my Lord, and God!

Sunset

In quiet evening beauty
A work of art flung high
With hues of rainbow colors,
    Sunset adorns the sky!

The flaming red grows fainter
A soft and gorgeous rose,
The pattern of such handwork?
    'Tis only God that knows.

The crimson glow has faded,
The first wee stars appear
I gaze in awe and wonder
    I feel His presence near.

(First published poem – August, 1963)